FURNITURE 1650~1800

COMPILED BY TONY CURTIS

ISBN 0-86248-014-0

Copyright © Lyle Publications MCMLXXXI
Published by Lyle Publications, Glenmayne, Galashiels, Selkirkshire, Scotland.

INTRODUCTION

This book is one of a series specially devised to aid the busy professional dealer in his everyday trading. It will also prove to be of great value to all collectors and those with goods to sell, for it is crammed with illustrations, brief descriptions and valuations of hundreds of antiques.

Every effort has been made to ensure that each specialised volume contains the widest possible variety of goods in its particular category though the greatest emphasis is placed on the middle bracket of trade goods rather than on those once-in-a-lifetime museum pieces whose values are of academic rather than practical interest to the vast majority of dealers and collectors.

This policy has been followed as a direct consequence of requests from dealers who sensibly realise that, no matter how comprehensive their knowledge, there is always a need for reliable, up-to-date reference works for identification and valuation purposes.

When using your Antiques and their Values Book to assess the worth of goods, please bear in mind that it would be impossible to place upon any item a precise value which would hold good under all circumstances. No antique has an exactly calculable value; its price is always the result of a compromise reached between buyer and seller, and questions of condition, local demand and the business acumen of the parties involved in a sale are all factors which affect the assessment of an object's 'worth' in terms of hard cash.

In the final analysis, however, such factors cancel out when large numbers of sales are taken into account by an experienced valuer, and it is possible to arrive at a surprisingly accurate assessment of current values of antiques; an assessment which may be taken confidently to be a fair indication of the worth of an object and which provides a reliable basis for negotiation.

Throughout this book, objects are grouped under category headings and, to expedite reference, they progress in price order within their own categories. Where the description states 'one of a pair' the value given is that for the pair sold as such.

The publishers wish to express their sincere thanks
to the following for their kind help and assistance
in the production of this volume:

JANICE MONCRIEFF
NICOLA PARK
CARMEN MILIVOYEVICH
ELAINE HARLAND
MAY MUTCH
MARGOT RUTHERFORD
JENNIFER KNOX

Printed by Apollo Press, Worthing, Sussex, England.
Bound by R. J. Acford, Chichester, Sussex, England.

CONTENTS

ARMOIRES

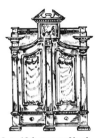

Mid 18th century Louis XV walnut provincial armoire, 4ft.9in. wide. $1,465 £650

Late 18th century North German or Scandinavian elm armoire, 84in. wide. $1,800 £800

18th century Spanish oak armoire with doors centred by roundels, 55½in. wide. $2,140 £950

Late 18th century French provincial walnut armoire, 4ft.10in. wide. $2,475 £1,100

17th century Dutch oak armoire, 220cm. wide. $3,095 £1,375

Mid 18th century French provincial oak armoire, 172cm. wide. $3,150 £1,400

Louis XV provincial armoire with two 19th century Japanese lacquer panels. $3,375 £1,500

Late 17th century Italian walnut armoire with carved frieze, 46in. wide. $3,375 £1,500

Early Louis XVI provincial armoire in chestnut, 5ft. wide. $4,050 £1,800

Early 18th century South
German walnut armoire, 80in. wide, with carved pediment.
$4,165 £1,850

Early 17th century North
German fruitwood and oak armoire. $4,950 £2,200

German armoire with carved and panelled doors.
$5,400 £2,400

Early 17th century German
marquetry armoire with
stepped pediment, 7ft.5in. wide. $5,625 £2,500

Late 18th century Dutch mar-
quetry armoire with shaped cornice, 6ft.3in. wide.
$5,625 £2,500

Late 16th century Flemish
walnut armoire, 5ft.6in. wide. $5,625 £2,500

Mid 18th century Dutch walnut armoire, 67½in. wide.
$9,450 £4,200

Dutch walnut and marque-
try armoire with arched
moulded cornice, 74in.
wide. $19,125 £8,500

18th century French armoire
in oak veneered with tor-
toiseshell, 1.47m. wide.
$30,375 £13,500

Late 18th century marquetry bed with scroll ends.
$1,465 £650

Hepplewhite mahogany four-poster bed with a dentil cornice.
$1,690 £750

Louis XVI carved walnut bed, 3ft.7½in. wide, circa 1790.
$1,690 £750

18th century Italian walnut four-poster bed.
$1,915 £850

18th century French bed, circa 1780, with shaped ends, canopy and bedspread, 8ft. 6in. high.
$2,475 £1,100

Italian painted pinewood bed, 4ft.8in. wide, circa 1690.
$2,815 £1,250

Early 17th century four-poster bed.
$3,490 £1,550

Partly 17th century oak four-poster bed, 6ft.10in. long.
$3,715 £1,650

Jacobean four-poster bed with hangings.
$5,065 £2,250

Elizabethan oak four-poster bed with panelled head-board. $5,850 £2,600

Chippendale mahogany low-post bedstead, 52in. wide. $6,190 £2,750

17th century carved oak four-poster bed, 4ft.6in. wide. $6,190 £2,750

George III four-poster bed. $7,090 £3,150

Carved oak four-poster bed with later additions. $7,650 £3,400

17th century tester bed with contemporary crewel work hangings. $11,250 £5,000

Elizabethan oak tester bed, 5ft.9in. wide, posts and backboard, circa 1600. $24,750 £11,000

Part of a neo-Gothic suite of bedroom furniture. $24,750 £11,000

Early George III carved gilt-wood and painted four-poster bed, 5ft.10in. wide, circa 1765. $37,125 £16,500

An oak bible box with lunette carving on the front, circa 1700. $225 £100

18th century Indo-Portuguese bible box in teak and ebony, 18½in. long.
$360 £160

An oak desk box with a hinged sloping front above stylised geometric carving, circa 1690. $450 £200

An oak bible box, showing the Stuart Coat of Arms, retaining the original hand-blocked lining paper.
$450 £200

Antique carved oak bible box with ground level stretchers. $475 £210

An oak bible box, its front and sides carved with two rows of flutings, with a reeded edge to the top, circa 1600. $790 £350

17th century oak bible box complete with stand.
$790 £350

Italian Renaissance casket, circa 1560, 1ft.10½in. wide. $2,080 £925

Charles I oak bible box, circa 1630, 2ft.3in. wide.
$3,940 £1,750

18th century carved oak bookcase, 114cm. wide.
$900 £400

George III mahogany bookcase, circa 1800, 3ft.11in. wide. $2,025 £900

George III mahogany bookcase with panelled cupboard to base, 3ft.4½in. wide. $2,365 £1,050

George II mahogany and parcel gilt bookcase, 67in. wide. $3,940 £1,750

George III figured and inlaid mahogany breakfront library bookcase.
$5,445 £2,420

George III satinwood breakfront library bookcase.
$14,625 £6,500

George III mahogany breakfront bookcase, probably designed by Robert Adam.
$25,875 £11,500

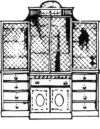

Sheraton satinwood breakfront cabinet, 7ft.1½in.
$40,500 £18,000

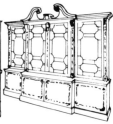

George III mahogany library bookcase by Thos. Chippendale, 1764.
$78,750 £35,000

13

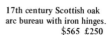

17th century Scottish oak arc bureau with iron hinges. $565 £250

Late 18th century oak bureau with mahogany banding and brass drop handles. $675 £300

Mid 18th century mahogany writing bureau with four drawers. $945 £420

George III country made oak and mahogany crossbanded bureau, 39in. wide. $1,170 £520

Mid 18th century Dutch colonial padoukwood bureau, 3ft.7½in. wide. $1,260 £560

Continental oak bureau, carved with cherubs and scrolls, 3ft.5in. wide. $1,575 £700

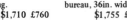

George III mahogany bureau with burr walnut and satinwood stringing. $1,710 £760

Early 18th century oak bureau, 36in. wide. $1,755 £780

Sheraton mahogany and inlaid bureau with four drawers, 39in. wide. $1,800 £800

18th century oak bureau with moulded decoration, 92cm. wide. $1,915 £850

Queen Anne walnut bureau, 3ft.4in. wide, circa 1710. $1,980 £880

Late 18th century Dutch mahogany cylinder bureau. $2,025 £900

Early George III mahogany bureau on stand, 3ft. wide. $2,475 £1,100

Italian walnut marquetry bureau, circa 1780, 4ft. 1in. wide. $2,475 £1,100

German black japanned writing cabinet, circa 1700, 3ft. 2in. wide. $2,590 £1,150

South African hardwood bureau made for the Cloets family in Cape Town. $2,700 £1,200

Queen Anne laburnum bureau, 3ft.2½in. wide. $2,700 £1,200

Queen Anne cedarwood bureau with sloping hinged lid, 40in. wide. $2,815 £1,250

15

18th century Dutch oak bureau with shaped front and paw feet. $2,925 £1,300

Dutch colonial tulipwood bureau with fall front. $3,150 £1,400

18th century walnut kneehole bureau with crossbanded flap. $3,150 £1,400

Late 18th century South Italian walnut bureau with slight serpentine front. $3,265 £1,450

Dutch marquetry bureau with shaped flap, on cabriole legs, 33in. wide. $3,600 £1,600

Dutch satinwood cylinder bureau, circa 1770, 3ft.6in. wide. $3,600 £1,600

South German walnut bureau with inverted serpentine lower part, circa 1750, 3ft. 4in. wide. $3,715 £1,650

Walnut and marquetry double cylinder bureau with two tambour fronts, Italian or Spanish, circa 1780, 6ft. wide. $3,940 £1,750

Mid 18th century George II walnut bureau on bracket feet, 3ft. wide. $3,940 £1,750

Louis XV provincial oak bureau a cylindre, circa 1770, 3ft.7in. wide.
$3,960 £1,760

Late 18th century Dutch bureau with fitted interior and three drawers.
$4,050 £1,800

German parquetry bureau with rectangular top, 29in. wide, on gilt metal mounted cabriole legs. $4,050 £1,800

Queen Anne walnut and crossbanded bureau in two parts, 86cm. wide.
$4,040 £1,800

18th century Dutch marquetry bureau with bombe base, 52in. wide. $4,390 £1,950

18th century Italian stained wood and mahogany cube parquetry fall front bureau.
$4,500 £2,000

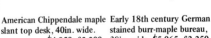

Mid 18th century Louis XV ormolu mounted parquetry cylinder bureau with tambour front, 4ft.3in. wide.
$4,950 £2,200

American Chippendale maple slant top desk, 40in. wide.
$4,950 £2,200

Early 18th century German stained burr-maple bureau, 38in. wide. $5,065 £2,250

George III mahogany and satinwood bureau, circa 1770, 3ft.6in. wide. $5,175 £2,300

Louis XV provincial walnut bureau, circa 1750, 3ft.7in. wide. $5,175 £2,300

18th century Flemish provincial bureau in carved oak. $5,625 £2,500

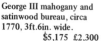

North Italian walnut and marquetry bureau with inlaid flap, late 18th century, 45½in. wide. $6,075 £2,700

Small early 18th century walnut bureau with fall front, 27in. wide. $5,625 £2,500

Dutch mahogany marquetry cylinder bureau, circa 1770, 4ft. wide. $6,190 £2,750

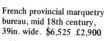

North Italian marquetry bureau, circa 1830, 3ft. 11in. wide. $6,525 £2,900

French provincial marquetry bureau, mid 18th century, 39in. wide. $6,525 £2,900

Lombard ivory inlaid walnut bureau, circa 1720. $6,930 £3,080

George I walnut bureau in need of repair.
$6,750 £3,000

Dutch marquetry cylinder bureau, circa 1775, 3ft.8in. wide. $6,975 £3,100

South German walnut bureau, circa 1740, 3ft. wide.
$8,100 £3,600

Mid 18th century Dutch marquetry bureau in walnut, 106cm. wide. $8,325 £3,700

Italian bureau de dame in walnut parquetry, inlaid with cedar, satinwood and tulipwood.
$8,550 £3,800

Queen Anne walnut kneehole bureau, 3ft.5in. wide, circa 1710. $9,450 £4,200

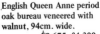

English Queen Anne period oak bureau veneered with walnut, 94cm. wide.
$9,675 £4,300

North Italian walnut marquetry and parquetry bureau with fitted interior.
$9,900 £4,400

18th century German walnut bureau cabinet with shaped front. $10,350 £4,600

Mid 18th century walnut bureau, 3ft.8in. wide.
$12,375 £5,500

George III satinwood and rosewood cylinder bureau.
$15,300 £6,800

George I cylinder bureau in burr yewwood.
$15,750 £7,000

William and Mary walnut seaweed marquetry bureau, 2ft. wide, circa 1690.
$17,100 £7,600

Cylinder bureau by C. C. Saunier, 3ft.4in. wide, circa 1780.
$54,000 £24,000

18th century Dutch mahogany and marquetry bureau.
$59,625 £26,500

Kingwood cylinder bureau by Oeben, 5ft.2in. wide.
$76,500 £34,000

Louis XV secretaire by Bernard II Van Risen Burgh, 26½in. wide.
$78,750 £35,000

Mid 18th century German ormolu mounted tulipwood and kingwood bureau, 37in. wide. $108,000 £48,000

Georgian mahogany fully fitted bureau bookcase with four graduated drawers. $2,250 £1,000

Late 18th century oak bureau bookcase on bracket feet. $2,700 £1,200

18th century mahogany bureau bookcase, carved and rebuilt, circa 1890. $2,815 £1,250

George III mahogany bureau bookcase, circa 1780, 3ft.6in. wide. $3,095 £1,375

Small walnut bureau cabinet, early 18th century, 1ft.8in. wide. $3,375 £1,500

Oak cylinder bureau cabinet, possibly German, circa 1780, 4ft.1in. wide. $3,375 £1,500

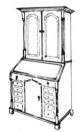

George III oak bureau cabinet, 3ft.2¾in. wide. $3,825 £1,700

18th century Georgian mahogany secretaire cabinet, 42in. wide. $3,825 £1,700

Inlaid mahogany bureau bookcase with glazed top. $3,940 £1,750

BUREAU BOOKCASES

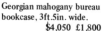

Georgian mahogany bureau
bookcase, 3ft.5in. wide.
$4,050 £1,800

Italian walnut bureau bookcase, lower part circa 1750,
3ft.8in. wide.
$4,500 £2,000

18th century mahogany bureau cabinet with moulded
dentil cornice, 39in. wide.
$4,500 £2,000

Queen Anne oak bureau cabinet, 3ft.8in. wide.
$4,500 £2,000

George III satinwood cylinder secretaire bookcase,
circa 1790, 3ft.2in. wide.
$4,500 £2,000

Venetian scarlet and cream
lacquer bureau cabinet, 49¼in
wide. $4,725 £2,100

North German mahogany
bureau bookcase, circa 1770,
4ft.4in. wide. $4,725 £2,100

George III mahogany cylinder bureau bookcase, circa
1780, 3ft.8in. wide.
$4,950 £2,200

18th century South German
oak and marquetry bureau
bookcase, 45in. wide.
$5,065 £2,250

Mid 18th century Dutch mahogany bureau cabinet, 4ft.1in. wide.
$5,400 £2,400

Chippendale style bureau cabinet with broken scrolled pediment, 53in. wide.
$5,850 £2,600

Mid Georgian oak bureau cabinet, 44in. wide.
$6,075 £2,700

Red lacquer double domed English bureau cabinet.
$6,750 £3,000

George III bureau bookcase in mahogany, 115cm. wide. $7,200 £3,200

George I red japanned bureau cabinet, 3ft.4in. wide.
$7,200 £3,200

Queen Anne walnut bureau bookcase, 37in. wide.
$8,665 £3,850

Queen Anne burr-walnut bureau bookcase, 26in. wide. $9,000 £4,000

George III mahogany bureau cabinet, circa 1780, 3ft.6½in. wide. $9,000 £4,000

BUREAU BOOKCASES

Late 18th century Dutch oak and floral marquetry bureau bookcase, 1.15m. wide.
$9,450 £4,200

German oak and walnut bureau cabinet with broken scrolled pediment, 47in. wide. $9,450 £4,200

William and Mary black lacquer double domed kneehole bureau cabinet, 3ft.9in. wide.
$9,565 £4,250

William and Mary oak bureau bookcase with twin domed top, 42in. wide.
$9,675 £4,300

George III mahogany bureau bookcase, 3ft.2in. wide, circa 1785.
$11,925 £5,300

George I walnut bureau cabinet with mirrored doors.
$13,050 £5,800

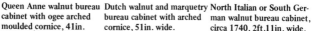

Queen Anne walnut bureau cabinet with ogee arched moulded cornice, 41in. wide. $13,500 £6,000

Dutch walnut and marquetry bureau cabinet with arched cornice, 51in. wide.
$14,625 £6,500

North Italian or South German walnut bureau cabinet, circa 1740, 2ft.11in. wide.
$15,750 £7,000

24

Queen Anne period bureau cabinet in oak veneered with walnut, 1.04m. wide.
$17,440 £7,750

Mid 18th century Venetian green lacquer bureau cabinet, 46in. wide.
$19,690 £8,750

Mid 18th century Sicilian bureau cabinet in walnut and marquetry, 1.07m. wide.
$21,375 £9,500

Walnut bureau cabinet, circa 1715, with mirrors on the outside of the doors, 47½in. wide.
$21,375 £9,500

Narrow Queen Anne bureau bookcase in burr walnut.
$33,415 £14,850

George I walnut bureau bookcase with broken circular pediment. $36,000 £16,000

George I figured walnut and carved parcel gilt bureau cabinet.
$40,500 £18,000

English scarlet lacquer bureau cabinet, circa 1715-20, 3ft. 5in. wide. $81,000 £36,000

Early 18th century bureau cabinet, circa 1730.
$126,000 £56,000

17th century German carved walnut cabinet, 64in. wide. $900 £400

17th century Flemish oak cabinet with fielded panels. $1,350 £600

George I black and gold lacquer cabinet on stand, 38in. wide. $1,690 £750

Flemish ebony cabinet, mid 17th century, 2ft.8in. wide. $2,250 £1,000

Late 18th century boulle filing cabinet, sides with Wedgwood plaques, 33½in. wide. $2,475 £1,100

George III mahogany cabinet on stand with marquetry panels on the doors. $2,475 £1,100

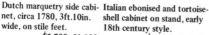

Dutch marquetry side cabinet, circa 1780, 3ft.10in. wide, on stile feet. $2,700 £1,200

Italian ebonised and tortoiseshell cabinet on stand, early 18th century style. $2,925 £1,300

Late 17th century Spanish walnut cabinet, 73in. wide. $3,095 £1,375

17th century Flemish oak cabinet on stand, dated 1630, 26in. wide. $3,150 £1,400

18th century Italian ebonised and marquetry chest on stand. $3,265 £1,450

Charles II black and gold lacquer cabinet on stand, 50in. wide. $3,375 £1,500

Carved walnut cabinet of Henry II style, 42in. wide. $3,375 £1,500

Late 17th century Indo-Portuguese rosewood and ebony marquetry cabinet on stand, 2ft.2½in. wide. $3,490 £1,550

18th century North Italian ebonised and Scagliola marble decorated cabinet on stand, 101cm. wide. $3,715 £1,650

Mid 17th century Spanish ebony cabinet on stand, 6ft. 2in. high. $3,780 £1,680

17th century carved oak cabinet, 3ft.10in. wide. $3,940 £1,750

Spanish walnut vargueno, 18th century, 2ft.9in. wide. $4,050 £1,800

CABINETS

17th century Austrian marquetry cabinet on stand, 31in. wide. $4,165 £1,850

Late 17th century Dutch colonial silver mounted cabinet on stand, 47cm. wide. $4,500 £2,000

17th century Italian walnut cabinet, 63½in. wide. $4,500 £2,000

Louis XV provincial oak cabinet on shaped feet, 50in. wide. $4,725 £2,100

Early 18th century burr walnut cabinet on stand with 16th century marquetry, 25¼in. wide. $4,840 £2,150

18th century Dutch floral marquetry cabinet on chest, 102cm. wide, with gilt metal fittings. $4,950 £2,200

William and Mary walnut cabinet on stand, 3ft.6½in. wide. $5,625 £2,500

Early George III mahogany side cabinet with serpentine top, circa 1765, 4ft. wide. $5,625 £2,500

Small William and Mary burr walnut cabinet on chest, 42in. wide. $5,625 £2,500

Late 17th century burr-elm cabinet on chest, 3ft.8in. wide. $6,300 £2,800

17th century bone and tortoiseshell Spanish cabinet on stand. $6,300 £2,800

Partly 17th century Dutch oak cabinet, 64in. wide. $6,750 £3,000

Antique Dutch oak marquetry cabinet, 3ft.5½in. wide, on stand. $6,750 £3,000

Early 18th century French red boulle bureau cabinet, 47in. wide. $6,750 £3,000

Late 18th century Dutch mahogany and marquetry cabinet, 5ft.3in. wide. $7,200 £3,200

Fine 18th century Dutch oak cabinet with shaped pediment. $7,200 £3,200

17th century Flemish ebony cabinet, 34in. wide. $7,200 £3,200

French Louis XV style silver display cabinet in marquetry, 158cm. wide. $7,200 £3,200

CABINETS

William and Mary seaweed marquetry cabinet on stand.
$7,315 £3,250

16th century Flemish oak Renaissance cabinet on stand. $7,425 £3,300

Flemish walnut cabinet on stand, circa 1670, 3ft.8in. wide, with giltwood cresting.
$7,425 £3,300

George III painted side cabinet, circa 1790, 5ft.6in. wide, with white marble top.
$7,650 £3,400

17th century Spanish walnut vargueno, 41½in. wide.
$8,440 £3,750

Queen Anne walnut cabinet on chest, 41½in. wide.
$9,000 £4,000

17th century Flemish carved oak cabinet, 44in. wide.
$9,000 £4,000

17th century Italian cabinet on stand in ebony with pietra dura panels, 1.31m. wide. $9,225 £4,100

Charles II lacquered and simulated tortoiseshell cabinet on stand. $9,450 £4,200

17th century Italian cabinet in pine, heavily carved.
$10,350 £4,600

18th century marquetry cabinet. $11,250 £5,000

Louis Phillipe marquetry satinwood and kingwood cabinet with ormolu mounts, 3ft.6in. wide.
$11,385 £5,060

James II red lacquered cabinet on silvered stand.
$14,400 £6,400

17th century Flemish oak side cabinet.
$32,625 £14,500

An early polychrome painted writing cabinet.
$51,750 £23,000

18th century satinwood and marquetry cabinet on stand. $67,500 £30,000

Early George III mahogany cabinet by Wm. Hallett, 53½in. wide.
$67,500 £30,000

17th century oak Flemish cabinet, heavily carved.
$74,250 £33,000

DINING CHAIRS

17th century English Flemish style side chair in yew and chestnut with cane seat and back. $205 £90

Oak hall chair, the back panel carved with hunting scene. $325 £145

George II mahogany hall chair with dished seat and curule legs. $360 £160

One of a pair of late 17th century walnut side chairs. $385 £170

German walnut revolving desk chair, circa 1785. $450 £200

One of two rush-seated spindleback dining chairs. $450 £200

One of a pair of 18th century oak and walnut Dutch hall chairs. $540 £240

Queen Anne walnut single chair with plain shaped splat back, front cabriole legs carved with foliage. $565 £250

One of a pair of 17th century Derbyshire chairs with solid panel seats. $565 £250

Mid 18th century Portuguese rosewood chair. $565 £250

One of a pair of 17th century chairs with solid panel seats. $575 £255

Late 18th century carved mahogany Chippendale style dining chair. $620 £275

One of six 18th century ash spindleback chairs with rush seats. $865 £385

One of a set of six inlaid mahogany chairs, circa 1790. $865 £385

One of a set of four North Italian fruitwood chairs, ivory inlaid, late 18th century. $1,170 £520

Fine Indo-Portuguese carved ebony chair, late 17th century. $1,170 £520

One of a set of six George III provincial elm dining chairs, circa 1800. $1,180 £525

One of a set of six American rush-seated stained elm and beech chairs, early 18th century. $1,180 £525

DINING CHAIRS

17th century walnut chair with carved frieze and stretcher. $1,240 £550

One of a pair of early 18th century mahogany framed chairs with crested pieces. $1,350 £600

One of a pair of Charles II walnut chairs, circa 1680 $1,465 £650

One of a pair of George II mahogany chairs, circa 1760. $1,530 £680

One of a set of six George III Hepplewhite dining chairs. $1,530 £680

Mid Georgian mahogany dining chair with waved top rail. $1,575 £700

One of a set of four early 18th century oak chairs with carved top rails. $1,690 £750

One of a set of six George III mahogany chairs, circa 1790. $1,845 £820

One of a set of six George III mahogany dining chairs, circa 1785. $2,250 £1,000

One of a set of six George III mahogany dining chairs.
$2,250 £1,000

One of a set of six George III mahogany dining chairs, circa 1780.
$2,260 £1,005

One of a set of eight 18th century Italian oak dining chairs with carved backs.
$2,700 £1,200

One of a pair of George I walnut dining chairs with slightly curved backs.
$2,815 £1,250

One of a set of six George III mahogany dining chairs, 32½in. high. $3,040 £1,350

One of eight similar fruit-wood chairs, late 17th century, possibly Flemish.
$3,095 £1,375

One of a set of six early George III mahogany dining chairs with Gothic pattern splats.
$3,375 £1,500

One of a set of six 17th century oak standard chairs.
$3,375 £1,500

One of a set of seven George III Irish mahogany ladder-back dining chairs.
$3,610 £1,605

DINING CHAIRS

One of a set of eight walnut dining chairs in William and Mary style. $3,825 £1,700

One of a set of twelve Chippendale mahogany dining chairs with pierced vase splats. $4,050 £1,800

One of a pair of George I walnut chairs with shaped front legs. $4,165 £1,850

One from a set of eight mahogany dining chairs on ball and claw feet. $4,500 £2,000

One of a set of six George III mahogany dining chairs, circa 1780. $4,500 £2,000

One of a set of six mid 18th century Dutch marquetry dining chairs with serpentine top rails. $4,500 £2,000

One of a set of four mid 18th century German cream painted chairs. $4,500 £2,000

One of a set of twelve Flanders neo-renaissance leather covered chairs. $4,725 £2,100

One of a set of six George III mahogany dining chairs. $5,625 £2,500

One of a set of eight George
III mahogany dining chairs
with comb splats.
$5,850 £2,600

One from a set of eight
Sheraton period mahogany
dining chairs.$6,300 £2,800

One of a set of six Queen
Anne walnut dining chairs.
$6,750 £3,000

One of a set of twelve Flemish
parcel gilt walnut chairs, circa
1690. $9,450 £4,200

One of a set of twelve early
18th century Italian giltwood chairs.
$9,675 £4,300

One of a set of ten George
III mahogany dining chairs.
$9,900 £4,400

One of a set of six George
II mahogany dining chairs,
possibly American.
$11,250 £5,000

One of a set of twelve
George III mahogany chairs,
circa 1785. $16,200 £7,200

One of a set of ten mahogany
chairs in the Chippendale
manner. $29,250 £13,000

ELBOW CHAIRS

Late 18th century elm Windsor stick back chair.
$225 £100

George I oak corner commode chair with shaped top rail. $250 £110

One of two provencal rush-seated elmwood fauteuils, late 18th century.
$450 £200

Early George III mahogany armchair, circa 1760.
$540 £240

18th century mahogany lattice back armchair, with upholstered seat.
$675 £300

Oak armchair with carved back and reeded stretchers.
$700 £310

George III mahogany armchair, circa 1785.$700 £310

Charles II oak armchair, circa 1680. $720 £320

Yew-wood high back Windsor elbow chair. $845 £375

38

Mid 18th century George III mahogany child's chair, 19½in. wide. $925 £410

One of a pair of late 18th century folding campaign chairs. $945 £420

Mahogany Chippendale ribbon back elbow chair on shaped legs. $1,035 £460

Carved oak wainscot chair with panelled back, 17th century. $1,060 £470

Early 17th century Spanish walnut armchair with leather back and seat. $1,080 £480

One of a pair of George II style walnut armchairs with ladder backs. $1,125 £500

Late 17th century Italian armchair with solid seat. $1,170 £520

18th century Chinese rosewood open armchair. $1,170 £520

Early 17th century oak box-seat with scratch-moulded back and shaped sides. $1,170 £520

ELBOW CHAIRS

Late George II padoukwood
corner armchair, circa 1755. 17th century Italian child's
$1,240 £550 oak high chair. $1,465 £650

Yew-wood and elm seat
baby's high chair.
$1,575 £700

17th century Spanish ebonised One of a pair of mid 18th Early 17th century oak wains-
open armchair, one of a pair. century Dutch armchairs. cot chair, with carved back.
$1,800 £800 $1,855 £825 $1,855 £825

George III mahogany armchair, 17th century turned oak
circa 1770. $1,915 £850 chair. $2,025 £900

George II library chair, upholstered in brass studded leather.
$2,025 £900

40

One of eight George I oak dining chairs, circa 1720.
$2,025 £900

One of a set of eight mid 18th century Dutch marquetry chairs.
$2,250 £1,000

Charles II open armchair, 1662, with curved arms.
$2,250 £1,000

One of a pair of George III painted armchairs, circa 1775.
$2,250 £1,000

One of a pair of Sheraton satinwood armchairs with shield backs, circa 1790.
$2,475 £1,100

Queen Anne walnut armchair with solid vase-shaped splat and needlework seat.
$2,590 £1,150

A Venetian giltwood throne, circa 1750, upholstered in velvet.
$2,590 £1,150

Gothic walnut armchair, 5ft.11in. high, circa 1500.
$2,700 £1,200

17th century oak wainscot chair with ground level stretchers.$2,925 £1,300

ELBOW CHAIRS

One of a pair of Spanish walnut open armchairs, basically 17th century. $2,925 £1,300

One of a set of eleven George III mahogany dining chairs. $3,150 £1,400

One of a set of eight early George III mahogany ladderback chairs, circa 1765. $3,375 £1,500

One of a rare set of five early George III mahogany hall chairs, circa 1760. $3,600 £1,600

Early 17th century oak wainscot armchair with carved back. $3,940 £1,750

One of a pair of mid 18th century Venetian painted armchairs. $4,275 £1,900

One of a pair of late George III mahogany armchairs, circa 1800. $4,725 £2,100

One of a pair of George III giltwood open armchairs with rounded arched backs. $5,175 £2,300

One of a pair of George III mahogany armchairs, circa 1765. $6,075 £2,700

Italian beechwood chair, circa 1740, one of a set of four.
$7,200 £3,200

One of a set of eight George III mahogany dining chairs, circa 1780. $7,650 £3,400

One of a pair of George I walnut corner chairs standing on pad feet.
$7,765 £3,450

One of a pair of mahogany armchairs, circa 1780.
$9,000 £4,000

Late Elizabethan oak and marquetry armchair, circa 1600. $9,000 £4,000

One of a set of eight, six singles and two arm, 18th century dining chairs.
$11,700 £5,200

One of a pair of mid 18th century yew and elmwood armchairs. $13,500 £6,000

One of a pair of English Queen Anne armchairs in walnut with needlework seat and back. $20,250 £9,000

One of a set of seven George I walnut dining chairs, circa 1725, including one armchair.
$21,600 £9,600

43

UPHOLSTERED CHAIRS

George III mahogany chair with padded arms, circa 1775. $565 £250

German carved beechwood fauteuil, circa 1740. $640 £285

Venetian giltwood armchair, circa 1700, with stuffed back. $865 £385

17th century oak adjustable wing back armchair. $1,015 £450

Fine George III mahogany saddle wing chair, 81cm. wide. $1,015 £450

Late 18th century mahogany framed Gainsborough chair. $1,200 £520

George III mahogany arm-chair, circa 1775. $1,395 £620

Late 17th century Italian walnut armchair with stuffed back and seat. $1,530 £680

Louis XV giltwood fauteuil by J. B. Boulard, 37in. high. $1,690 £750

UPPER CHAIRS

French or Flemish walnut armchair, circa 1680. $1,970 £875

George II mahogany armchair with serpentine top back, circa 1750. $2,140 £950

Early Louis XV walnut fauteuil with arched back, circa 1730. $2,205 £980

Mid 18th century North Italian carved giltwood sleigh seat. $2,475 £1,100

Mid 18th century German blue and pink painted fauteuil. $2,815 £1,250

One of a pair of Low Countries Louis XVI walnut fauteuils. $2,925 £1,300

One of a pair of mid 18th century Venetian painted armchairs with drop-in seats. $3,375 £1,500

Old open armchair of the George I period with carved paw feet. $4,275 £1,900

George III mahogany library armchair of Chippendale style, arm supports carved with foliage. $4,500 £2,000

UPHOLSTERED CHAIRS

Louis XVI mahogany fauteuil
de bureau, circa 1785.
$4,725 £2,100

Late 17th century walnut
open framed armchair.
$4,725 £2,100

James II wing chair with
elaborately carved scroll-
work, circa 1685.
$5,625 £2,500

George II mahogany library
armchair, circa 1755, back
broken. $5,850 £2,600

Charles II giltwood arm-
chair, with carved front
stretcher. $6,750 £3,000

George I open armchair with
arched padded back and
bowed seat. $7,200 £3,200

One of a pair of Hepplewhite
armchairs with mahogany
frames. $7,425 £3,300

One of a pair of Regency
giltwood caned fauteuils,
circa 1715.
$11,250 £5,000

Bergere by Jean-Baptiste Sene,
circa 1789. $65,250 £29,000

18th century oak chest of drawers with brass loop handles and mahogany crossbanding. $225 £100

George III mahogany chest of three drawers, 92cm. wide. $630 £280

George III oak chest of drawers, circa 1790, 20¼in. wide. $730 £325

Late 17th century oak chest of four long drawers, 100cm. wide. $845 £375

George III mahogany chest of drawers, circa 1770, 3ft. 1¼in. wide. $900 £400

Jacobean oak chest with a pair of geometrically moulded doors, 3ft.3in. wide. $1,035 £460

Late 17th century oak carved chest, 4ft.3in. wide. $1,070 £475

William and Mary walnut chest of drawers, circa 1690, 3ft. wide. $1,125 £500

17th century oak chest of drawers, 42in. wide. $1,170 £520

CHEST OF DRAWERS

George II mahogany bachelor's chest, circa 1740, 3ft. wide. $1,295 £575

George II mahogany linen press and chest, 3ft.1in. wide, circa 1760.
$1,295 £575

Small George III serpentine fronted mahogany chest, 3ft.3in. wide, circa 1785.
$1,575 £700

Late George III satinwood chest of drawers, top crossbanded with rosewood, 35½in. wide. $1,690 £750

Jacobean oak chest of four long drawers, 98cm. wide.
$1,690 £750

Inlaid chest of four long drawers, circa 1670, Anglo-Dutch, in oak and softwood, 3ft.6in. wide. $1,845 £820

Charles II oak chest, 3ft.2in. wide, circa 1670.
$2,140 £950

George II walnut chest of drawers with marquetry inlay, 38in. wide.
$2,925 £1,300

Small 17th century oak chest of drawers, 31in. wide.
$3,150 £1,400

Late 17th century South German walnut and inlaid chest, decorated with hunting scenes, 142cm. wide. $3,265 £1,450

Anglo-Dutch penwork decorated walnut chest of five drawers, 3ft.3in. wide, circa 1700. $3,265 £1,450

Charles II walnut and marquetry chest, 39in. wide. $3,375 £1,500

Mid 17th century inlaid oak chest, circa 1650, 3ft. 8in. wide. $3,490 £1,550

William and Mary marquetry chest of four drawers. $3,490 £1,550

17th century Italian inlaid chest of four drawers, veneered in fruitwood, 4ft. 10in. wide. $3,715 £1,650

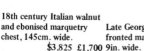

18th century Italian walnut and ebonised marquetry chest, 145cm. wide. $3,825 £1,700

Late George II serpentine fronted mahogany chest, 3ft. 9in. wide. $3,940 £1,750

Hepplewhite period bow fronted chest of drawers, 3ft.1½in. wide. $4,050 £1,800

Late 18th century lacquer chest, 26in. wide. $4,050 £1,800

Dutch marquetry chest of drawers, circa 1760, 3ft.1in. wide. $4,050 £1,800

William and Mary oyster walnut chest of five drawers, 3ft. 5in. wide. $4,165 £1,850

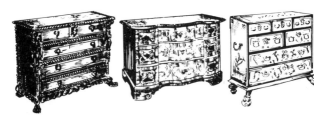

Late 16th century Italian walnut chest, 3ft.8in. wide. $4,165 £1,850

Mid 18th century German walnut chest of drawers, 42in. wide. $4,840 £2,150

Late 17th/early 18th century Goanese inlaid chest of drawers, 4ft.3in. wide. $4,950 £2,200

Jacobean yew-wood chest of drawers with brass drop handles. $5,290 £2,350

Small serpentine fronted chest of drawers in mahogany. $5,625 £2,500

William and Mary oyster walnut chest with satinwood crossbanding. $5,965 £2,650

Sheraton period mahogany bow fronted dressing commode. **$6,075 £2,700**

Early 18th century Italian walnut chest, 70½in. wide. **$6,190 £2,750**

Charles II oak chest of drawers, 3ft.1½in. wide, circa 1660. **$6,190 £2,750**

Late 18th century North Italian marquetry chest of three drawers. **$6,525 £2,900**

Late George II walnut chest of three drawers, with brushing slide, circa 1760, 2ft.8in. wide. **$7,650 £3,400**

Anglo-Dutch chest of two short and three long drawers, circa 1700. **$9,000 £4,000**

William and Mary marquetry chest of drawers. **$9,000 £4,000**

18th century Central European walnut serpentine chest of three drawers. **$13,950 £6,200**

Queen Anne walnut bachelor's chest, early 18th century. **$18,000 £8,000**

51

CHEST ON CHEST

George III oak tallboy, circa 1780, 3ft.10in. wide.
$675 £300

George III mahogany bow fronted tallboy, 104cm. wide.
$1,150 £510

Late 18th century flame mahogany chest on chest on ogee feet. $1,240 £550

Late 18th century oak chest on chest.
$1,350 £600

Late 18th century Irish mahogany tallboy on claw feet.
$1,510 £670

Mid 18th century mahogany chest on chest.
$1,800 £800

Georgian walnut tallboy, slightly restored, on bracket feet.
$2,250 £1,000

William and Mary cabinet on chest fitted with central cupboard.
$2,925 £1,300

17th century oak chest in two sections, decorated all over, 38in. wide.
$3,150 £1,400

George I walnut tallboy on bracket feet.
$3,375 £1,500

George III mahogany tallboy, circa 1780, 3ft.11in. wide.
$4,500 £2,000

Queen Anne period walnut crossbanded and herring-bone inlay tallboy chest, 3ft.4¼in. wide.
$4,500 £2,000

18th century country made walnut tallboy, 3ft.2in. wide.
$4,950 £2,200

18th century mahogany chest on chest fitted with brushing slide.
$5,850 £2,600

Dutch marquetry tallboy, 3ft.4in. wide, circa 1700.
$6,300 £2,800

18th century Queen Anne burr walnut cabinet on chest, 109cm. wide.
$7,200 £3,200

Early George III mahogany tallboy, 49¼in. wide, on later scrolled. feet.
$8,550 £3,800

George I walnut tallboy, base with secretaire drawer, 42½in. wide.
$15,300 £6,800

Small oak chest on stand with moulded drawer fronts, 52in. high, circa 1780.
$900 £400

Late 18th century cross-banded chest on stand.
$1,015 £450

Early 18th century walnut chest on stand.
$1,125 £500

17th century Spanish chest on carved stand.
$1,120 £520

Late 17th century country made chest on stand in oak.
$1,575 £700

17th century oak chest on stand, 38in. wide.
$1,915 £850

Continental red walnut chest on stand with basket weave carving, 48in. wide.
$2,025 £900

George I oak and walnut chest on stand, 3ft.4¾in. wide, circa 1720.
$2,080 £925

Portuguese rosewood chest on stand, 40¾in. wide.
$2,250 £1,000

Dutch or Swedish oak chest on stand, circa 1660, 3ft.8in. wide. $2,475 £1,100

Early 18th century chest on stand in oyster walnut veneer inlaid with floral marquetry. $3,825 £1,700

George I oak and walnut tallboy on cabriole legs. $4,050 £1,800

Walnut Queen Anne chest on stand, circa 1689, 3ft. 6in. wide. $4,950 £2,200

A Queen Anne mulberry wood chest on stand with onion shaped feet. $5,065 £2,250

William and Mary oyster veneered walnut cabinet on stand, 3ft.2in. wide, circa 1695. $5,175 £2,300

Late 17th century Flemish ebonised and decorated chest on stand. $9,900 £4,400

Queen Anne maple highboy, 38½in. wide, circa 1730-60.$11,700 £5,250

Charles II period walnut veneered chest on stand, with marquetry decoration, 5ft. 3in. high, 48½in. wide, 1ft. 8in. deep, circa 1685. $16,875 £7,500

COFFERS & TRUNKS

Late 18th century pine coffer on bracket feet. $145 £65

Late 18th century dark green leather hide covered coaching trunk, 36in. long. $370 £165

18th century oak dower chest, dated 1742. $450 £200

17th century carved oak coffer, 120cm. wide. $640 £285

18th century Indian Indo-Portuguese blanket chest, heavily carved, 58in. long. $720 £320

Oak mule chest, dated 1705, with two side cupboards and two drawers. $790 £350

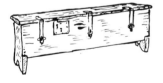

Early 17th century oak chest, 3ft.9in. wide. $925 £410

Oak linen chest, circa 1660, 5ft. wide. $925 £410

17th century ark-top chest, 4ft.9½in. wide.
$1,035 £460

Heavily carved 17th century oak coffer with panelled front. $1,035 £460

George II black japanned chest, mid 18th century, with later stand, 4ft.1½in. wide. $1,170 £520

Early 17th century oak coffer, German or Scandinavian, 3ft.9in. wide. $1,260 £560

17th century oak coffer, inscribed 'MP 1593', 52in. wide. $1,305 £580

Dutch Colonial nadun wood chest, 40in. wide. $1,405 £625

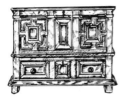

Mid 17th century oak mule chest with rising top, 4ft.2¾in. wide. $1,465 £650

Late 17th/early 18th century leather painted chest with domed top, 3ft.2in. wide. $1,485 £660

COFFERS & TRUNKS

Small 15th century plank built oak coffer with original lock plate, 40in. wide. $1,575 £700

Early 17th century Italian cassone in walnut, 2ft.7in. high x 5ft.8in. wide. $1,630 £725

17th century oak and yew small coffer on gothic arcaded trestle supports, 30in. wide. $2,025 £900

Small 16th century oak linen fold coffer with plank top, 28½in. wide.
$2,025 £900

Queen Anne black japanned coffer, circa 1710, 5ft.3in. wide.
$2,025 £900

Mid 18th century brass mounted chest of the East India Company, 3ft.8in. wide.
$2,250 £1,000

Carved oak chest, circa 1540, 3ft.4in. wide. $2,250 £1,000

Georgian black and gold lacquer coffer on stand, 50in. wide. $2,250 £1,000

17th century Italian walnut coffer.
$2,475 £1,100

Early 17th century James I oak chest on
stile feet, 3ft.10½in. wide. $2,815 £1,250

Rare 17th century oak domed top ark
of plank construction, 97cm. wide.
$2,880 £1,280

Gothic oak coffer with rectangular top,
circa 1520, 4ft.1in. wide. $3,600 £1,600

16th century oak coffer of panelled construction. $3,715 £1,650

George II walnut and mahogany chest
with hinged lid, circa 1740, 3ft.9in. wide.
$3,715 £1,650

Late 15th century Piedmontese walnut cassone, 4ft.8in. wide. $6,750 £3,000

An oak chest, 5ft.9in. wide, circa 1480.
$11,815 £5,250

COMMODES & POT CUPBOARDS

18th century mahogany commode in the form of a chest of four drawers with brass handles, 56cm. wide.
$80 £35

18th century oak commode with dummy drawers.
$370 £165

Late 18th century mahogany, tambour fronted, night commode, with carrier handles.
$450 £200

Late 18th century George III mahogany tray top bedside table. $595 £265

Late 18th century Chippendale style mahogany night table, 23in. wide, with tray top.
$675 £300

18th century marquetry bedside cupboard, 2ft.6in. high.
$730 £325

Late 18th century satinwood bedside table on square tapering legs. $1,125 £500

French directoire bidet with marble top, 52cm, wide.
$5,625 £2,500

Night table of Marie Antoinette, 38in. high, 1784.
$61,875 £27,500

French walnut commode, circa 1790, 43½in. wide. $865 £385

18th century Dutch serpentine burr-wood commode, 44in. wide. $1,915 £850

Small Louis XVI commode in walnut and kingwood, 1ft.9½in. wide. $1,970 £875

Mahogany commode, circa 1750, 3ft.2in. wide, possibly German. $2,025 £900

Danish walnut and giltwood commode in two parts, 4ft. 2in. wide, circa 1750. $2,590 £1,150

Late 18th century German walnut commode, 52½in. wide. $2,700 £1,200

North Italian serpentine commode, late 18th century. $3,600 £1,600

18th century Dutch walnut and floral marquetry commode with shaped top. $3,825 £1,700

Scandinavian walnut marquetry chest, circa 1780, 3ft.11½in. high. $4,085 £1,815

COMMODE CHESTS

Louis XV provincial walnut serpentine fronted commode, 3ft.11in. wide. $5,065 £2,250

Late 18th century Italian rosewood and marquetry commode. $5,400 £2,400

North Italian walnut commode, circa 1770, 4ft. 7½in. wide. $5,400 £2,400

George III mahogany commode, 3ft.4½in. wide, circa 1770. $5,850 £2,600

Louis XV marquetry commode by A. Levesque, 51¼in. wide. $7,200 £3,200

18th century Danish walnut and parcel gilt bombe commode, 78cm. wide. $10,125 £4,500

Lombard ivory inlaid walnut commode, circa 1760, 4ft. 3in. wide. $10,350 £4,600

Louis XV commode in veneerwood, signed Desforges, Paris, circa 1750. $11,545 £5,130

Louis XV commode in marquetry decorated with fire gilt bronze, after Duplessis Pere. $14,400 £6,400

German or Austro-Hungarian walnut parquetry commode, circa 1760, 3ft.9¾in. wide. $16,875 £7,500

George III satinwood and marquetry commode, 53¼in. wide. $22,500 £10,000

Louis XIV marquetry and ormolu mounted commode, 122cm. wide. $30,940 £13,750

Louis XV/XVI transitional ormolu mounted marquetry commode, stamped C. Wolff. $37,125 £16,500

Louis XIV boulle commode inlaid in marquetry on a ground of scarlet tortoiseshell. $37,125 £16,500

Two-drawer commode by Simon Oeben. $60,750 £27,000

One of a pair of George III marquetry commodes by Wm. Moore, Dublin, circa 1780, 4ft.5in. wide. $69,750 £31,000

Louis XIV boulle commode chest. $175,500 £78,000

George III ormolu mounted commode by Pierre Langlois, 5ft.1in. wide, circa 1760. $270,000 £120,000

Late 18th century pine corner cupboard of good colour. $205 £90

Late 18th century mahogany hanging corner cupboard. $450 £200

George III walnut veneered corner cupboard with swan neck pediment, $565 £250

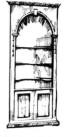

George I black lacquer hanging corner cabinet, 36½in. high. $675 £300

George III stripped pine corner cupboard with shaped shelves. $790 £350

Georgian domed corner cupboard, circa 1740. $1,125 £500

Late 18th century inlaid mahogany corner cupboard. $1,125 £500

Georgian mahogany corner display cabinet, 3ft.6in. wide. $1,430 £635

Georgian corner cabinet in mahogany. $2,475 £1,100

Carved and painted corner cupboard with pierced cornice, circa 1760, 2ft. 5in. wide. $2,475 £1,100

Dutch kingwood and purple-heart encoignure, 3ft.2½in. wide, circa 1760.
$2,700 £1,200

One of a pair of Italian rococo parcel gilt painted corner cupboards.
$3,825 £1,700

One of a pair of South German kingwood and tulip-wood standing corner cupboards, mid 18th century.
$5,175 £2,300

George I mahogany corner cupboard, 4ft. wide.
$5,625 £2,500

18th century walnut double corner cupboard, 246cm. high. $6,075 £2,700

One of a pair of late 18th century mahogany cabinets with shaped marble tops.
$6,750 £3,000

18th century Dutch marquetry corner cupboard.
$11,250 £5,000

One of a pair of mid 18th century Louis XV ormolu mounted kingwood parquetry encoignures, 3ft.0½in. high. $15,750 £7,000

COURT CUPBOARDS

James I oak court cupboard, circa 1620, 5ft.wide.
$1,395 £620

17th century carved oak court cupboard.
$1,465 £650

17th century French oak dressoire with geometric inlay and blind fret decoration, 52in. wide.
$2,025 £900

18th century oak court cupboard with potboard, 4ft. wide. $2,025 £900

17th century oak court cupboard, 61in. wide.
$2,125 £945

Mid 17th century oak court cupboard with carved frieze, 4ft.6in. wide.
$2,250 £1,000

18th century oak court cupboard, 56½in. wide.
$2,475 £1,100

Late 17th century Welsh oak duodarn, 48in. wide.
$2,475 £1,100

Queen Anne oak court cupboard, circa 1710, 4ft.3in. wide. $2,590 £1,150

18th century oak court cupboard with fielded panel doors. $2,700 £1,200

Early 18th century oak tridarn, 53in. wide, with fielded cupboard doors. $2,925 £1,300

Commonwealth oak court cupboard with moulded cornice, 67in. wide. $2,925 £1,300

Late 17th century Welsh oak court cupboard. $3,825 £1,700

Mid 17th century carved and panelled oak court cupboard. $3,825 £1,700

Continental court cupboard with fitted drawer and under tray. $4,500 £2,000

Commonwealth oak court cupboard with moulded rectangular top, 44½in. wide, inlaid with bone and mother-of-pearl. $4,950 £2,200

George II oak and elm court cupboard, 3ft.7in. wide, circa 1735. $7,425 £3,300

Continental oak court cupboard, heavily carved and of good size. $10,350 £4,600

CRADLES

Late 18th century mahogany crib. $340 £150

A Normandy carved oak cradle with openwork end bobbin panels, 3ft.4in. wide. $450 £200

Dutch child's cradle in the form of a sledge, 22in. long. $675 £300

Oak cradle with carved lunettes and lozenge decoration. $675 £300

17th century Continental oak crib. $730 £325

Early 17th century hooded oak baby's cradle. $790 £350

17th century carved oak hooded cradle. $1,350 £600

Kidney-shaped Empire style child's cradle, circa 1800, 39in. long. $1,575 £700

17th century oak cradle with pointed hood, 3ft. long. $1,800 £800

17th century Italian walnut cupboard with single panel door, 68cm. wide.
$295 £130

17th century French carved oak cupboard, 65cm. wide.
$395 £175

18th century mahogany clothes press with two drawers.
$520 £230

Mid 17th century oak cupboard, 4ft.1in. wide.
$900 £400

Early 18th century oak cupboard, 55in. wide.
$1,125 £500

French walnut food hutch, circa 1780. $1,125 £500

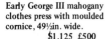

Early George III mahogany clothes press with moulded cornice, 49½in. wide.
$1,125 £500

Old carved oak cheese cupboard, heavily carved, 3ft. 5in. wide. $1,170 £520

Early English livery cupboard in oak with wrought iron hinges, 23½in. wide.
$1,305 £580

CUPBOARDS

17th century Flemish carved oak cupboard, 122cm. wide. $1,305 £580

English livery cupboard in carved oak with inlaid panels, 3ft.2½in. wide. $1,420 £630

18th century oak settle with panelled cupboard doors. $1,440 £640

Mid 18th century oak cupboard on chest, 186cm. wide. $1,530 £680

Charles I oak food cupboard. $1,610 £715

Late 17th/early 18th century Dutch colonial aramana wood cupboard, 4ft.5in. wide. $1,690 €750

Commonwealth oak cupboard, 4ft.3in. wide, circa 1650. $1,800 £800

Early Louis XV provincial oak cupboard, 3ft.10in. wide, circa 1730. $1,845 £820

Georgian oak bacon cupboard on bracket feet. $1,915 £850

Mid 18th century Louis XV provincial oak cupboard, 4ft.8in. wide. $2,025 £900

18th century Continental carved oak bacon cupboard, 200cm. wide. $2,250 £1,000

Antique Flemish carved oak cupboard, 5ft.4in. wide. $2,250 £1,000

17th century Flemish cupboard, dated 1650, 150cm. wide. $2,475 £1,100

17th century carved oak cupboard, 4ft.7in. wide. $2,590 £1,150

18th century Dutch mahogany linen press, 66in. wide. $2,815 £1,250

South German marquetry cupboard on chest, circa 1740, 2ft.11½in. wide. $2,815 £1,250

18th century Normandy Regency bridal cupboard in oak. $2,925 £1,300

Flemish oak cupboard, circa 1650, 5ft.3in. wide. $3,150 £1,400

CUPBOARDS

George III mahogany clothes press, 51in. wide.
$3,150 £1,400

Charles II oak and walnut chest. $3,195 £1,420

18th century oak Breton cupboard, 59in. wide.
$3,265 £1,450

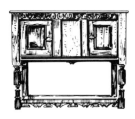

Early 17th century Flemish or German oak cupboard, 3ft.9in. wide.
$3,375 £1,500

Early 17th century James I oak livery cupboard.
$4,275 £1,900

17th century South German walnut and inlaid side cupboard. $4,275 £1,900

17th century English oak hall cupboard with iron hinges. $4,950 £2,200

German walnut parquetry cupboard, circa 1740, 6ft. 2in. wide. $5,625 £2,500

15th century Gothic oak food cupboard with pierced and carved front, 49in. wide.
$6,300 £2,800

A Bavarian carved walnut cupboard, 7ft. wide.
$6,750 £3,000

Dutch mahogany clothes press, with stepped pediment, circa 1780, 6ft.10in. wide. $6,750 £3,000

17th century Netherlands renaissance style cupboard in ebony and walnut veneer.
$6,750 £3,000

16th century North European carved oak dressoir.
$7,425 £3,300

Unique 17th century part open cupboard, 66½in. wide. $9,450 £4,200

Early 18th century Dutch four-door rosewood and ebony cupboard.
$9,565 £4,250

18th century Dutch walnut and marquetry cupboard and stand, 73¼in. wide.
$10,350 £4,600

17th century Flemish oak cupboard, 68¾in. wide.
$14,625 £6,500

French marquetry and parquetry Louis XVI cupboard, stamped Reisener.
$40,500 £18,000

DISPLAY CABINETS

Finely carved late 18th century Oriental hardwood display cabinet. $900 £400

George II red walnut display cabinet, circa 1740, 3ft.7in. wide.
$1,125 £500

18th century satinwood display table, 17in. wide.
$1,745 £775

18th century Dutch walnut display cabinet with shaped pediment. $2,250 £1,000

18th century French provincial pine buffet, 55in. wide. $2,250 £1,000

Georgian mahogany china display cabinet, 31½in. wide with glazed doors.
$2,925 £1,300

George III mahogany book or display case, 4ft.9in. wide, circa 1780. $3,040 £1,350

Walnut and parcel gilt cabinet on stand with glazed top, 40in. wide.
$3,150 £1,400

18th century Liege carved oak display cabinet.
$5,040 £2,240

18th century Dutch marquetry display cabinet, 36½in. wide. $5,850 £2,600

Mahogany display cabinet with broken triangular pediment, 47in. wide, mid 18th century. $6,300 £2,800

Louis XV silver display cabinet with gilt bronze mounts. $6,525 £2,900

Late 18th century Dutch walnut display cabinet. $6,750 £3,000

Early George III mahogany display cabinet, 4ft. wide. $6,750 £3,000

Early 18th century Dutch mahogany and marquetry display cabinet, 5ft.6in. wide. $9,000 £4,000

Mid 18th century Dutch marquetry display cabinet. $11,250 £5,000

Dutch floral marquetry display cabinet with bombe front. $14,625 £6,500

Dutch marquetry display cabinet with arched moulded cornice, 84½in. wide. $20,250 £9,000

DRESSERS

18th century French provincial oak buffet, 124cm. wide. $360 £160

Small mahogany dresser base with two drawers, 48in. wide. $620 £275

Oak dresser with waved frieze and open shelves, 65½in. wide. $1,395 £620

18th century Lancashire oak and pine dresser. $1,800 £800

An 18th century Irish pine-wood dresser, the base with three silhouette shaped front legs, the three drawers having brass handles, circa 1750. $1,800 £800

18th century oak dresser with pierced cornice, 97in. wide. $1,845 £820

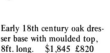

Early 18th century oak dresser base with moulded top, 8ft. long. $1,845 £820

Honey coloured 18th century oak dresser with spice drawers, 50in. wide. $1,855 £825

Georgian oak low dresser with moulded rectangular top crossbanded in mahogany, 73½in. wide. $1,915 £850

Flemish 17th century oak dresser fitted with three drawers, 7ft. long.
$1,980 £880

Charles II oak dresser with dentil mounted and pierced cornice, circa 1665, 6ft.3in. wide. $2,025 £900

Mid 18th century oak dresser base, 5ft.6in. wide.
$2,025 £900

18th century French provincial oak buffet, 58¼in. wide.
$2,250 £1,000

George III oak dresser with plate racks, 5ft.7in. wide. $2,475 £1,100

18th century oak dresser with moulded rectangular top, 84in. wide.
$2,475 £1,100

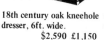

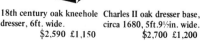

18th century oak kneehole dresser, 6ft. wide.
$2,590 £1,150

Charles II oak dresser base, circa 1680, 5ft.9½in. wide.
$2,700 £1,200

Late George II oak dresser, 5ft. wide, circa 1760.
$2,700 £1,200

DRESSERS

Late Georgian Welsh oak dresser, 72in. wide.
$2,815 £1,250

George III oak dresser, circa 1780, 6ft.4in. wide.
$2,815 £1,250

George II oak and elm dresser with moulded cornice, 4ft. 7½in. wide, circa 1750.
$2,815 £1,250

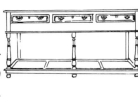

Antique oak small dresser, 4ft. 8½in. wide. $2,970 £1,320

Early 18th century country made oak dresser, 72in. wide. $2,845 £1,265

German dark oak dresser with three cupboard doors to the base. $3,265 £1,450

Early 18th century chestnut dresser, known as a buffet-vaisselier, 55in. wide.
$3,375 £1,500

18th century oak clock dresser, dial signed Nathaniel Olding, Wincanton, 96in. wide.
$3,375 £1,500

Anglesey dresser in oak banded with mahogany. $3,465 £1,540

Mid 18th century oak dresser, rack with cavetto cornice, 6ft. wide.
$3,600 £1,600

18th century French provincial oak dresser.
$3,715 £1,650

Late 17th century oak dresser with open shelves.
$3,715 £1,650

Late 18th century oak dresser base, 5ft.11in. wide.
$4,275 £1,900

James I oak buffet with parquetry drawer at top, circa 1610, 4ft. wide.
$6,075 £2,700

Small Jacobean oak dresser base. $6,075 £2,700

18th century French provincial oak dresser, 80in. wide.
$8,550 £3,800

Late 17th century yewwood dresser base, 5ft. 11in. wide.
$12,150 £5,400

Louis XV decorated cartonnier in fruitwood.
$12,375 £5,500

DUMB WAITERS

George II mahogany dumb waiter, 24in. diameter. $450 £200

George III mahogany dumb waiter, circa 1790. $900 £400

Mid 18th century mahogany dumb waiter with a capstan top. $900 £400

Chippendale period mahogany graduated three-tier dumb waiter, circa 1770, 43in. high. $945 £420

George III mahogany three-tier dumb waiter, circa 1760, 43in. high. $1,270 £565

George III mahogany four-tier dumb waiter of faded colour on a three branch pedestal, circa 1790. $1,350 £600

George II mahogany dumb waiter with two circular tiers, 2ft.2½in. wide, circa 1745. $1,620 £720

George III three-tier mahogany dumb waiter on a tripod base with ball and claw feet. $1,800 £800

George III mahogany dumb waiter, 3ft.3½in. high, circa 1785. $2,025 £900

Late 18th century carved oak lowboy, 3ft. wide.
$280 £125

Late 18th century mahogany lowboy with original brass fittings. $620 £275

Georgian lowboy in mahogany with brass handles.
$845 £375

Mid 18th century oak lowboy on four cabriole legs, 80cm. wide. $1,125 £500

Late 18th century mahogany lowboy on square cut cabriole legs. $1,350 £600

18th century Dutch marquetry lowboy, 84cm. wide.
$1,465 £650

George II mahogany lowboy with four drawers, circa 1735, 2ft.6in. wide.
$2,815 £1,250

Queen Anne lowboy, with original handles missing and veneer damaged.
$3,825 £1,700

Queen Anne cherrywood lowboy, circa 1750, 33in. wide.
$16,875 £7,500

Late 18th century mahogany writing desk with nine drawers, 3ft.6in. wide.
$565 £250

18th century mahogany kneehole desk, 32in. wide.
$1,015 £450

18th century mahogany kneehole writing desk.
$1,215 £540

Early 18th century mahogany kneehole desk, 32in. wide.
$1,610 £715

Chippendale kneehole desk, circa 1770, 3ft.9in. wide.
$1,630 £725

Late 18th century inlaid mahogany cylinder desk, 44in. wide. $2,700 £1,200

George III mahogany kneehole desk with cloth lined top, 47½in. wide.
$2,700 £1,200

A George III mahogany architect's kneehole desk with an adjustable top, 3ft. 2in. wide. $2,815 £1,250

18th century fruitwood kneehole desk of fine golden colour, 2ft.11in. wide.
$2,925 £1,300

George II padoukwood knee-hole writing table with leather writing surface, 2ft.11½in. wide. $3,040 £1,350

George III partner's desk in mahogany, 4ft. wide, circa 1790. $3,825 £1,700

An unusual 18th century walnut kneehole desk on bracket feet. $3,940 £1,750

Georgian mahogany fall flap kneehole bureau on ogee feet. $3,940 £1,750

An 18th century English burr yew partner's desk on paw feet. $4,500 £2,000

Late 18th century Sheraton inlaid and decorated satin-wood kneehole desk. $4,500 £2,000

George II mahogany knee-hole writing table, circa 1745, 2ft.8½in. wide. $5,175 £2,300

North Italian rosewood knee-hole desk, top crossbanded with tulipwood, 52in. wide. $5,400 £2,400

William and Mary period walnut kneehole desk with ebony arabesque marquetry inlay. $5,625 £2,500

One-piece mahogany pedestal writing desk, circa 1760, 81cm. wide. $2,625 £2,500

George III mahogany desk, circa 1765, 6ft.6¼in. wide open. $6,750 £3,000

Continental kneehole desk in parquetry applied walnut, circa 1680, with hinged top, 43in. wide. $7,425 £3,300

George II mahogany kneehole desk with serpentine top, 44½in. wide.$10,125 £4,500

George II mahogany kneehole desk, 3ft.2in. wide, circa 1760.
$13,500 £6,000

George II mahogany kneehole desk with leather lined top, 49½in. wide.$21,375 £9,500

Louis XIV boulle mazarin. $22,500 £10,000

An 18th century Massachusetts kneehole writing desk in mahogany.
$22,500 £10,000

The Combe Abbey library table in mahogany, by Thos. Chippendale.
$247,500 £110,000

Late 18th century mahogany framed firescreen with embroidered silk. $280 £125

Late 18th century giltwood firescreen with needlework panel. $340 £150

A pair of turned and carved mahogany pole firescreens, circa 1790, 59in. high. $1,070 £475

Louis XVI painted leather screen, 6ft.6in. high, circa 1780. $1,465 £650

18th century Dutch painted leather six-leaf screen, 97in. high. $3,150 £1,400

Mid 18th century Louis XV decoupage six-leaf screen. $3,150 £1,400

18th century Chinese draught screen, 1.88m. high. $6,750 £3,000

Mid 18th century Dutch leather six-fold screen, 96in. high. $9,450 £4,200

Louis XVI giltwood screen with eight panels. $10,125 £4,500

George II period red walnut secretaire, 4ft.1in. wide. $945 £420

Mahogany secretaire of the Sheraton period, interior with concave drawers and inlay, 43in. high, circa 1800. $1,350 £600

Italian walnut secretaire a abattant, 2ft.9in. wide, circa 1790. $1,405 £625

18th century oak fall front escritoire on chest. $1,465 £650

Walnut veneered fall front cabinet of William and Mary design, 40in. wide. $3,095 £1,375

Dutch marquetry secretaire a abattant, circa 1780, 3ft. wide. $3,265 £1,450

Queen Anne walnut and featherbanded escritoire, 112cm. wide. $4,165 £1,850

16th century Spanish walnut vargueno, 4ft.2in. wide. later stand. $4,500 £2,000

18th century Dutch satinwood and sycamore secretaire, 2ft. wide. $4,725 £2,100

George I burr-walnut secretaire chest on chest, 3ft. 8½in. wide, circa 1720.
$5,175 £2,300

Hepplewhite mahogany secretaire inlaid with rosewood and satinwood.
$5,400 £2,400

Late 17th century Dutch oak secretaire cabinet, 58in. wide. $5,625 £2,500

Late George II mahogany secretaire cabinet attributed to Thos. Chippendale, 96in. high. $8,440 £3,750

William and Mary marquetry secretaire, 3ft.10½in. wide, circa 1695.
$10,350 £4,600

Good Liege secretaire cabinet in burr-elm with ebonised and walnut banding, circa 1730, 3ft.11in. wide.
$11,250 £5,000

Louis XV period French secretaire a abattant in oak.
$15,750 £7,000

Satinwood fall front secretaire by J. H. Reisener, circa 1780, 55½in. high.
$38,250 £17,000

French secretaire a abattant in oak veneered with tulipwood and kingwood, 58cm. wide, by Jean-Francois Dubot. $90,000 £40,000

George III country oak secretaire bookcase, circa 1790, 3ft.6½in. wide. $1,405 £625

Georgian mahogany secretaire bookcase on shaped bracket feet.
$1,575 £700

Late 18th century rosewood secretaire bookcase.
$2,475 £1,100

George III mahogany secretaire bookcase, 44in. wide.
$4,165 £1,850

Georgian secretaire cabinet, 4ft.6in. wide.
$4,455 £1,980

Chippendale period mahogany secretaire bookcase with ogee feet. $4,500 £2,000

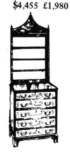

George III mahogany serpentine fronted secretaire bookcase, 120cm. wide.
$5,400 £2,400

George III mahogany secretaire open bookcase, 81cm. wide. $6,300 £2,800

George III mahogany small secretaire bookcase, circa 1770, 2ft.7½in. wide.
$6,300 £2,800

George III mahogany secretaire bookcase, 7ft.7½in. high, 4ft.1in. wide.
$7,315 £3,250

Queen Anne walnut secretaire cabinet, 2ft.5in. wide, circa 1710, on later bun feet.
$8,100 £3,600

George III mahogany library breakfront secretaire bookcase.
$10,350 £4,600

Late 17th century green lacquered double domed secretaire cabinet, 1.04m. wide.
$10,460 £4,650

Sheraton period secretaire cabinet, veneered in mahogany and banded with rosewood.
$11,250 £5,000

English secretaire cabinet, circa 1780, veneered with sycamore, rosewood and fruitwood, 1.2m. wide.
$11,250 £5,000

George III mahogany breakfront secretaire bookcase.
$24,750 £11,000

Sheraton period secretaire bookcase.
$24,750 £11,000

George III satinwood and marquetry library secretaire bookcase, 92in. wide.
$39,375 £17,500

18th century oak triple chair-back settee, 62in. wide. $790 £350

18th century carved oak settle with hinged lid. $1,035 £460

Chippendale period mahogany framed settee, 5ft.2in. long. $1,240 £550

Early George III three chair-back settee, 5ft.5in. wide. $1,240 £550

17th century box seat settle in oak, 105cm. wide. $1,240 £550

Louis XV beechwood canape on moulded cabriole legs, 5ft.1in. wide. $1,405 £625

Mahogany framed Hepplewhite design and period settee with fluted arms, 6ft. 4in. wide. $1,465 £650

Carved oak bench from 15th century panels, 5ft.5in. long. $1,465 £650

Queen Anne walnut settee, 3ft.1in. wide, circa 1710. $1,745 £775

Late 18th century George III grey-painted sofa, 72in. wide. $1,855 £825

Louis XVI gilt canape with petal-moulded frame, 4ft.5in. wide. $1,855 £825

Late George II walnut chair-back settee, 4ft.1in. wide, circa 1750. $1,915 £850

16th/17th century French Gothic oak bench, 5ft.11in. wide, with carved front panelling. $2,025 £900

Louis XV giltwood veilleuse, 70¾in. long. $2,250 £1,000

Louis XVI oak lit d'alcove, 6ft.7in. long, circa 1785. $2,250 £1,000

17th century oak settle with high panelled back and open scroll arms, dated 1648. $3,490 £1,550

SETTEES & COUCHES

Venetian rococo green-painted and parcel gilt settee, circa 1760, 3ft.2in. wide. $3,715 £1,650

Early Louis XV grained beechwood canape, 77½in. wide, with triple arched back. $4,050 £1,800

Queen Anne walnut settee, circa 1710, 6ft.8in. wide, worked in wool and silk petit point. $4,950 £2,200

Charles II walnut day bed, circa 1660, 5ft. long with caned back. $5,400 £2,400

George II mahogany sofa with triple arched back, circa 1755, 6ft.9in. wide. $5,850 £2,600

Queen Anne walnut settee on cabriole legs, 59in. wide. $6,525 £2,900

Louis XVI carved boxwood canape, circa 1780, 5ft. wide, stamped Delaisement. $14,175 £6,300

George III mahogany framed settee by T. Chippendale, 47½in. wide. $33,750 £15,000

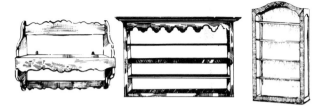

Pinewood kitchen mortar rack to hold two mortars, circa 1780, 23½in. wide. $85 £38

Late 18th century oak two-shelved hanging plate rack. $170 £75

Yew-wood hanging display cabinet of Queen Anne style, 23in. wide. $395 £175

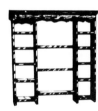

George III turned mahogany hanging bookshelves, 33in. wide. $395 £175

An oak Delft rack, circa 1740, 46in. wide x 45½in. high. $505 £225

Chippendale style mahogany wallshelves with fretted sides, circa 1760. $505 £225

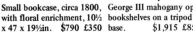

Small bookcase, circa 1800, with floral enrichment, 10½ x 47 x 19½in. $790 £350

George III mahogany open bookshelves on a tripod base. $1,915 £850

One of a pair of late George III giltwood eagle wall brackets, circa 1800, 1ft.3in. high. $4,275 £1,900

18th century mahogany chest sideboard inlaid in the Sheraton manner. $675 £300

Adam mahogany serving table with concave flanks and bow fronts, 8ft. wide. $855 £380

Late 18th century padoukwood pedestal sideboard. $1,125 £500

18th century French provincial sideboard, 5ft. wide, 3ft.2in. high, 2ft. deep. $1,465 £650

George III Scottish mahogany serpentine fronted sideboard, circa 1790, 7ft.3in. wide. $1,465 £650

George III mahogany small sideboard with rectangular top, 34in. wide. $1,755 £780

George III mahogany bow front sideboard on reeded legs. $1,970 £875

George III satinwood breakfronted serving table, 71in. wide. $2,250 £1,000

George III mahogany sideboard, 60¼in. wide.
$3,265 £1,450

Small breakfront mahogany sideboard,
circa 1780, 4ft.4in. wide. $3,375 £1,500

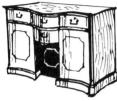

Chippendale period mahogany sideboard. $4,725 £2,100

Sheraton mahogany serpentine front sideboard
complete with a pair of knife urns.
$5,625 £2,500

George III mahogany sideboard, with reeded
projecting corners and original brass knobs.
$6,750 £3,000

Attractively figured Sheraton serpentine
fronted sideboard. $6,750 £3,000

George III semi-circular mahogany sideboard, circa 1785, 3ft.6in. wide.
$7,200 £3,200

Late 18th century Sheraton mahogany sideboard with inlaid ovals. $12,375 £5,500

95

STANDS

Louis XV style double tier etagere with marble top, 33cm. wide. $450 £200

American country string quartet music stand, 50in. high, circa 1800.
$495 £220

William and Mary walnut candle stand, late 17th century, 3ft.3in. high. $540 £240

Early 18th century walnut linen press, 5ft. high.
$675 £300

Mid 18th century mahogany jardiniere, 28¾in. high.
$1,465 £650

George II mahogany reading stand, the adjustable top with candle stand, circa 1740.
$1,630 £725

One of a pair of oak Solomonic torcheres, 75in. high.
$1,745 £775

One of a pair of George III mahogany torcheres, 38¾in. high. $4,725 £2,100

18th century French gueridon in parquetry and inlay, with silk lined drawer.
$13,050 £5,800

George III antique oak steps, circa 1790, 17¼in. wide, original bracket feet.
$215 £95

Georgian mahogany bed steps fitted with a cupboard and bidet drawer, the steps in green leather with gilt embossing, 1ft.9in. wide, 2ft.3in. high.
$565 £250

Late 18th century mahogany library steps on short turned legs.
$620 £275

George III mahogany library steps with brass fittings.
$790 £350

Set of George III folding library steps, 7ft.5½in. high, open. $955 £425

Set of George III mahogany library steps in the shape of a side table, 29½in. wide.
$2,250 £1,000

Early 18th century Italian prie dieu inlaid with ivory.
$2,815 £1,250

Mahogany eight tread library steps with handrails, converting to a rectangular top table, on chamfered legs, 40in.
$4,500 £2,000

George III oak and satinwood library steps, 7ft.8in. high. $7,425 £3,300

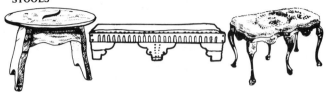

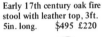

Small late 17th century
elm stool with an oval
top. $80 £35

Early 17th century oak fire
stool with leather top, 3ft.
5in. long. $495 £220

Dutch walnut and marquetry
duet stool, upholstered in
floral tapestry. $495 £220

Queen Anne oak close
stool with simulated
drawers. $620 £275

17th century oak joint
stool. $790 £350

George I walnut stool with
drop-in seat, 1ft.9in. wide,
circa 1720. $810 £360

Mid 18th century rectangular
gilt gesso stool, 23in. wide.
            $1,125 £500

One of a pair of George
II mahogany stools, 1ft.
10in. wide. $1,295 £575

James I oak joint stool, circa
1610, 1ft.6in. wide.
            $1,520 £675

Queen Anne walnut oval
stool with cabriole legs and
club feet. $1,755 £780

A window seat in the Chippendale manner with scrolled ends and gros-point
needlework, 4ft. long.
            $1,800 £800

Late 16th century Italian walnut stool, top with cut-out
handle, 1ft.4¼in. wide.
            $1,800 £800

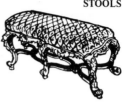

Charles II walnut stool, 3ft. 3in. wide, circa 1680.
$2,250 £1,000

Late 18th century North Italian rosewood and marquetry prieu dieu, 22¾in. wide. $2,250 £1,000

Early 18th century German giltwood banquette, 44in. wide. $2,815 £1,250

One of a pair of George I walnut stools, circa 1710, 1ft. 8½in. wide. $4,500 £2,000

Chippendale mahogany stool, circa 1760, 18½in. high. $4,500 £2,000

Henry VIII oak joint stool, 1ft.6in. wide, circa 1540, top restored. $4,825 £2,145

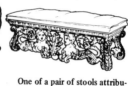

16th century oak box stool. $6,300 £2,800

One of a pair of fine Queen Anne stools, 17½in. high. $10,690 £4,750

One of a pair of stools attributed to Wm. Kent, of carved giltwood, 1.4m. wide. $16,312 £7,250

Wooden stool from the Austral Islands, probably Tahiti, 22in. wide. $19,125 £8,500

One of a pair of folding stools by Jean-Baptiste Sene, circa 1786. $121,758 £54,115

Stool by a 'Master of Buli', West Africa, Luba. $540,000 £240,000

A late 18th century giltwood three-piece suite, in the French style.
$5,175 £2,300

An Adam style drawingroom suite comprising circle back settee, four dining chairs and two armchairs, with the frames painted, carved and fluted.
$5,625 £2,500

Part of a set of eight mahogany chairs and a settee. $8,550 £3,800

Part of a nine-piece suite, settee 54½in. wide. $10,350 £4,600

Part of a set of twelve George II seat furniture. $12,375 £5,500

Near matching suite of Queen Anne furniture consisting of eight chairs and walnut settee. $18,000 £8,000

Part of a French giltwood chateau suite of Louis XV design, comprising a canape, four fauteuils, banquette stool, firescreen and three-fold screen.
$22,500 £10,000

Suite of South German marquetry seat furniture, mid 18th century.
$37,125 £16,500

CARD & TEA TABLES

Late 18th century country Chippendale mahogany tea table, 72cm. wide.
$450 £200

George II red walnut tea or games table, circa 1740, 2ft.8in. wide.
$745 £330

George III mahogany fold-over table of serpentine form, 94cm. wide.
$990 £440

George II semi-circular mahogany card table, 1ft. 8in. wide, circa 1740.
$1,295 £575

Georgian mahogany card table, on cabriole legs, 2ft.4in. wide.
$1,295 £575

18th century Dutch walnut and marquetry half-moon card table, 2ft.7in. high.
$1,405 £625

18th century concertina-action tea table in mahogany, with finely carved cabriole legs on ball and claw feet. $2,025 £900

Late 18th century walnut card table with baize lined top, legs overlaid with brass, 36in. wide. $2,140 £950

George II mahogany card table with concertina leg action, circa 1730.
$2,250 £1,000

Late George II mahogany card table, circa 1755, 2ft. 11½in. wide. $2,365 £1,050

Hepplewhite mahogany card table, 3ft. wide, on French cabriole legs.
$3,600 £1,600

Sheraton mahogany and branch satinwood card table, 35½in. wide, circa 1800.
$4,050 £1,800

Late 17th century walnut games table with fold-over top, 33in. long.
$4,725 £2,100

Early 18th century George II mahogany triple top games table, 33¼in. wide.
$4,725 £2,100

Charles II oak gateleg games table, circa 1670, 2ft.9in. diam. $5,200 £2,310

Mid 18th century Dutch marquetry walnut games table on pad feet. $6,020 £2,675

One of a pair of satinwood card tables, circa 1785.
$8,440 £3,750

18th century inlaid walnut centre table with circular recesses for gaming counters.
$11,815 £5,250

Italian painted consol table on hoof feet, circa 1790. $675 £300

George II painted consol table, 3ft.5½in. wide. $1,465 £650

Giltwood consol table with marble top, probably Scandinavian, circa 1770, 2ft.8in. wide. $1,575 £700

Early 18th century George I giltwood consol table, 48in. wide. $1,855 £825

Mid 18th century German white painted and parcel gilt consol table, 27½in. wide. $2,700 £1,200

Louis XV giltwood consol table with brown and white marble top, 40½in. wide. $4,500 £2,000

Early 18th century German carved oak consol table. $4,500 £2,000

Mid 18th century Genoese painted consol table, 4ft. 1in. wide. $5,625 £2,500

Giltwood consol table, circa 1765, by Robt. Adam. $29,250 £13,000

Jacobean style oak draw-leaf dining table, 7ft. long extended. **$1,170 £520**

Late 18th century mahogany breakfast table on quadruple base. **$1,600 £710**

17th century Flemish oak draw-leaf table on bulbous legs. **$2,250 £1,000**

Louis XV drawingroom table in satinwood, 29in. high. **$2,475 £1,100**

17th century German walnut centre table. **$2,700 £1,200**

18th century satinwood table inlaid with bog wood. **$3,375 £1,500**

Early 17th century Italian walnut table, 41¾in. diam. **$5,400 £2,400**

George II mahogany rent table with twelve drawers, 4ft.6in. diam. **$6,300 £2,800**

George III mahogany rent table, 42in. diam. **$13,500 £6,000**

DRESSING TABLES

Small late 18th century bow-fronted mahogany dressing table. $1,070 £475

George III mahogany dressing table with real and dummy drawers below. $1,350 £600

Late 18th century gentleman's bow-fronted mahogany chest of drawers, 42in. wide. $1,575 £700

Georgian red walnut dressing table with rising top, 2ft.7in. wide. $1,575 £700

Sheraton period mahogany 'D' table, 36in. wide, circa 1780. $1,745 £775

Fitted satinwood kneehole dressing table, 35in. wide. $2,250 £1,000

Queen Anne black and gold lacquer union suite with bureau base, 21½in. wide. $2,925 £1,300

Georgian mahogany dressing and writing table, 36in. wide, 23in. deep, 31in. high. $4,500 £2,000

Louis XV kingwood and tulipwood parquetry coiffeuse, 3ft. 1in. wide, circa 1760. $8,100 £3,600

George II mahogany oval
gateleg table, 104cm. wide.
$495 £220

Dutch mahogany and marquetry drop-leaf table, circa 1760,
4ft. wide. $1,015 £450

17th century Italian walnut
centre table. $1,800 £800

Rare yew-wood envelope
table with flap supported by
a loper, circa 1730.
$2,025 £900

George II mahogany drop-
leaf table, circa 1740, 3ft.
11½in. wide.
      $2,250 £1,000

17th century oak well table
on turned legs.$2,250 £1,000

Italian walnut drop-leaf table,
circa 1610, 3ft.11½in. long.
$2,475 £1,100

Dutch marquetry gateleg
dining table, 51in. wide.
       $3,960 £1,760

Queen Anne maple drop-leaf
dining table, 36in. diam., on
cabriole legs. $5,625 £2,500

GATELEG TABLES

Mid 17th century oak gateleg table, 36in. wide. $765 £340

Mid 17th century carved oak gateleg table, 72in. wide, open. $790 £350

17th century oak gateleg table with fitted single drawer. $855 £380

17th century oak gateleg table, circa 1670, 26½in. diam. $1,225 £545

Late 17th century oak oval gateleg dining table, 4ft.8½in. opened. $1,240 £550

William and Mary oak gateleg table, circa 1690, 4ft. 6in. open. $1,405 £625

Charles II oak gateleg table, 3ft.1in. wide, circa 1680. $1,465 £650

Louis XIV walnut double gateleg table, circa 1680, 4ft. 11in. open. $1,690 £750

Charles II oak gateleg table, 4ft. wide, circa 1665. $1,835 £815

Charles II small oak gateleg table, circa 1685, 2ft.8in. wide. $2,025 £900

Small 17th century oak gateleg table of oval form, 42in. wide, open.
$2,105 £935

Charles I oak gateleg table, circa 1640, 5ft.6in. extended.
$2,250 £1,000

Charles II large oak gateleg table, circa 1680, 5ft.10in., open. $3,715 £1,650

Charles II oak gateleg table, circa 1670, 3ft.2in. wide. $3,960 £1,760

17th century oak double gateleg table. $4,050 £1,800

William and Mary turned maple gateleg table, 48in. long. $4,500 £2,000

Charles II oak oval gateleg table, circa 1680, 4ft.10in. wide. $5,065 £2,250

17th century large oak gateleg table on turned legs.
$8,100 £3,600

109

LARGE TABLES

18th century D-ended mahogany dining table.   **$1,890 £840**

17th century oak and beechwood centre table, 83in. long.   **$2,250 £1,000**

Early 18th century Continental walnut dining table on shaped legs, 6ft. long.   **$2,475 £1,100**

George III D-ended mahogany dining table, 9ft.9in. long extended.   **$2,700 £1,200**

Georgian mahogany three part D-ended dining table, 90in. long, circa 1770.   **$2,815 £1,250**

Single plank oak trestle-end dining table, 8ft.2in. long, with single stretcher.   **$3,490 £1,550**

Early 17th century oak dining table, 73½in. wide.   **$3,715 £1,650**

Early 17th century Dutch oak draw-leaf table, 7ft.7in. wide, open. **$4,500 £2,000**

George III mahogany hunting table, 8ft.
10in. long, circa 1780. $4,500 £2,000

Early 17th century Italian walnut centre
table, 65in. wide. $4,500 £2,000

17th century Florentine walnut refectory
table, 7ft.6in. long. $6,750 £3,000

17th century Flemish pale oak draw-leaf
dining table, 90in. long.$7,425 £3,300

George II mahogany two pedestal dining
table, circa 1760, 5ft.6in. long.
                             $11,250 £5,000

17th century Swiss walnut draw-leaf table
on turned baluster legs. $12,940 £5,750

Mid 17th century Emilian walnut table,
probably Bologna, 6ft.2½in. long.
                             $14,850 £6,600

Elizabethan oak draw-leaf refectory table,
2ft.10in. wide. $25,875 £11,500

111

18th century elm cricket table. $100 £45

18th century mahogany circular tray topped table on tripod base. $315 £140

18th century walnut chateau wine tasting table with folding top. $340 £150

George II mahogany small table with cabriole legs, 27in. high. $340 £150

George III mahogany circular supper table, 29½in. diam. $675 £300

Solid walnut centre table, circa 1740, 2ft.9in. wide, possibly Portuguese. $900 £400

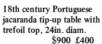

18th century Portuguese jacaranda tip-up table with trefoil top, 24in. diam. $900 £400

17th century Italian walnut, marquetry and ivory inlaid table, 48in. wide. $1,170 £520

Louis XV circular occasional table, veneered in tulipwood and parquetry inlay, 25¾in. diam. $1,170 £520

18th century Oriental padouk centre table, 52½ x 23in.
$1,260 £560

Dutch painted tripod table with octagonal top, circa 1740, 2ft.3in. wide.
$1,400 £620

18th century carved walnut centre table with marble top, 47in. wide. $1,690 £750

George III mahogany architect's table, circa 1765, 2ft. 11½in. wide. $1,690 £750

George III satinwood vide poche, 2ft. wide.
$2,025 £900

George III mahogany drum top table, 3ft.7in. diam.
$2,025 £900

Late George II mahogany tripod table, 2ft. high.
$2,250 £1,000

Late 17th century Spanish walnut table.$2,700 £1,200

Chippendale period mahogany architect's table.
$3,375 £1,500

113

Marquetry centre table, stretchers edged with bone and ebony, 45in. wide. $3,375 £1,500

James I oak hutch table, circa 1620, 2ft.8in. wide. $3,375 £1,500

German ormolu mounted marquetry poudreuse, 2ft. 4in. wide, circa 1750. $4,050 £1,800

Early George III mahogany tripod silver table, circa 1760, 2ft.2in. diam.$4,275 £1,900

Late 18th/early 19th century Russian Karelian birch, marquetry and parquetry table a rognon, 3ft. 1in. wide. $4,500 £2,000

Small George II marble topped red walnut table, 1ft. 10in. wide. $5,625 £2,500

Mid 18th century Louis XV marquetry coiffeuse, 2ft.4½in. high. $11,810 £5,250

Late 17th century Flemish table, the legs formed as classically draped men and women, 3ft.5in. long. $22,500 £10,000

18th century marquetry table in two sections, 2ft. 3½in. wide. $289,950 £128,870

George III faded mahogany and crossbanded rectangular Pembroke table, 77cm. wide. $790 £350

George III mahogany 'butterfly' shaped Pembroke table, 2ft.6in. wide, circa 1780. $1,240 £550

Mahogany Pembroke table of Hepplewhite design, 29in. wide. $1,575 £700

Early George III laburnumwood veneered Pembroke table, 3ft.4in. wide. $1,630 £725

George III mahogany supper table, with wire grills to the lower section, 39¾in. wide. $2,140 £950

George III satinwood Pembroke table, circa 1780, 2ft. 10in. wide. $2,250 £1,000

Late 18th century Dutch marquetry circular drop-leaf table, circa 1790, 4ft.10in. diam. $3,265 £1,450

George III satinwood 'Harlequin' Pembroke table, 36¼in. wide, open. $10,690 £4,750

George III mahogany 'butterfly' shaped Pembroke table, 37½in. wide, open. $14,625 £6,500

SIDE TABLES

Late 18th century oak side table on square legs. $110 £50

Antique walnut side table with three drawers, 3ft.6in. wide. $675 £300

Late 17th century oak side table, 33in. wide. $1,125 £500

George II mahogany side table, 4ft.5½in. wide. $1,240 £550

George III solid yew-wood table, circa 1770, 2ft.6½in. wide. $1,460 £650

George III satinwood side table, 51¾in. wide. $1,460 £650

One of a pair of Louis XVI pier tables, 18th century, French, 36in. wide. $1,750 £775

Dutch marquetry side table, circa 1750, 2ft.8in. wide. $1,750 £775

James I oak side table with bulbous supports, circa 1610. $1,800 £800

116

Rare 18th century Portuguese colonial side table, 29¼in. high. $2,025 £900

George II walnut side table, 2ft.6in. wide, circa 1730. $2,140 £950

18th century black lacquer side table with tray top, 2ft. 6in. wide. $2,250 £1,000

Mid 18th century South German giltwood side table, 59¼in. wide. $2,250 £1,000

16th century oak side table with deep drawer and shaped plank supports. $2,475 £1,100

Charles II walnut side table, 2ft.10in. wide, circa 1680, possibly Flemish. $2,700 £1,200

Mid 18th century Dutch walnut marquetry side table with shaped top. $2,815 £1,250

Bavarian giltwood side table, Munich, circa 1725, 4ft.2½in. wide, later marble top. $3,040 £1,350

Unusual William and Mary oak side table, 26in. high. $3,825 £1,700

SIDE TABLES

17th century Spanish walnut
side table, 46in. wide.
$3,825 £1,700

Dutch marquetry serpentine
side table, 35in. wide.
$3,940 £1,750

James I oak side table, circa
1620, 3ft.0½in. wide.
$3,940 £1,750

George I gilt gesso side table,
in need of restoration.
$7,875 £3,500

18th century giltwood
side table on square
tapered legs.
$9,000 £4,000

Highly carved George II
giltwood side table.
$9,000 £4,000

Louis XIV boulle side table,
4ft.10in. wide.
$12,710 £5,650

George I walnut side table,
top and oak lined drawer
crossbanded with feathered
inlay. $13,500 £6,000

18th century marble topped
Louis XVI marquetry table.
$19,125 £8,500

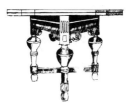

George III satinwood oval work table, circa 1790, 1ft. 6in. wide. $1,170 £520

17th century Flemish oak games table, 42in. wide, on three bulbous supports. $2,250 £1,000

Dutch marquetry semi-circular games table with sliding centre leg, 28½in. high. $2,250 £1,000

Sheraton period tulipwood tricoteuse of French influence, 27 x 16in. $2,810 £1,250

George III satinwood work table, 1ft.8in. wide, circa 1790. $3,490 £1,550

Late 17th century walnut games table on turned legs. $5,625 £2,500

Late 18th century mahogany games and writing table, 75 x 109 x 56cm. $5,625 £2,500

17th century South German games table complete with games. $12,375 £5,500

Russian ebony and boulle games table, late 18th century, 30½in. wide. $45,000 £20,000

Late 18th century French carved oak bonheur du jour, 40in. wide. $675 £300

Custom Hepplewhite mahogany tambour desk, 35½in. wide, with satinwood inlay. $1,430 £635

Sheraton design satinwood and tulipwood crossbanded reading table, 22in. wide. $1,745 £775

Louis XV style rosewood bonheur du jour. $2,140 £950

Louis XVI writing table in satinwood and mahogany with brass bandings, 2ft. wide. $2,250 £1,000

Early 18th century North Italian walnut writing table. $2,700 £1,200

George III satinwood bonheur du hour on square tapering legs, 2ft.3in. wide. $4,165 £1,850

Early 17th century South German walnut marquetry writing table, 2ft.7in. high. $5,175 £2,300

George III satinwood writing table with tambour top, circa 1785, 2ft.6in. wide. $6,300 £2,800

Louis XVI style bonheur du jour in kingwood marquetry, circa 1770. $9,450 £4,200

Louis XIV boulle bureau mazarin. $12,600 £5,600

Genoese walnut parquetry writing table with serpentine top, 5ft.10in. wide, circa 1760. $13,500 £6,000

Louis XV parquetry bonheur du jour, stamped L. Boudin, 31½in. wide. $20,250 £9,000

Louis XIV floral marquetrey bureau-plat. $28,125 £12,500

Ormolu mounted mahogany bonheur du jour, circa 1780, 2ft.3½in. wide. $29,250 £13,000

Late 18th century library table in mahogany and oak, 146cm. long. $32,175 £14,300

Transitional bonheur du jour by Piognez. $32,400 £14,400

Small writing table signed de Joseph. $270,000 £120,000

WASHSTANDS

George III mahogany square toilet stand, circa 1790, 32in. high. $280 £125

Georgian mahogany washstand with folding top. $395 £175

Georgian corner washstand decorated in green and gold Chinese lacquer. $530 £235

Late 18th century mahogany washstand with folding top. $620 £275

Sheraton period corner toilet stand, circa 1790, 43¾in. high. $665 £295

Sheraton period mahogany toilet stand inlaid with ebony stringing, 22in. wide. $665 £295

A mahogany powdering stand, with two drawers and undershelf, on cabriole legs, 3ft.10in. high. $900 £400

George III mahogany washstand, 24in. wide. $1,070 £475

George III colonial padouk-wood toilet table with divided hinged top, 2ft.1in. wide. $1,240 £550

Chippendale mahogany cushioned top cellarette with fitted interior and brass carrying handles. $925 £410

Early 18th century Sinhalese hardwood and ebony wine cooler, 2ft.7in. wide. $1,090 £485

Late 18th century Dutch marquetry oval wine cooler, 1ft.8½in. wide. $1,970 £875

George III cellarette with domed lid, 1ft.9in. wide, circa 1785. $1,980 £880

Brass bound mahogany wine cooler. $2,025 £900

George III brass bound mahogany wine cooler with twin carrying handles, 11in. wide. $2,365 £1,050

George III serpentine fronted mahogany cellarette, circa 1760, 1ft.6in. wide. $3,490 £1,550

Georgian oval brass bound wine cooler. $4,500 £2,000

George III mahogany wine cooler with brass liner and brass bound body, 23in. wide. $10,350 £4,600

INDEX